Spell with Zip

Zip

Zip is a friendly space alien from planet Zee. He loves to learn. Zip uses his hands to speak to his friends. He can't wait to teach the people of planet Earth all about sign language. Zip is the captain of his spaceship.

Pella

Pella is Zip's best friend. She also comes from planet Zee. Pella is very brave. Although she is a little younger than Zip and Statz, she isn't afraid of anything and is always the first of the three friends to try new things.

Statz

Statz is in charge of computers on the spaceship. He loves gadgets. Statz uses his Zablet to help him and his friends out of sticky situations. He is excited to learn about planet Earth and all the people who live here.

Goober

Goober is an unexpected guest on the friends' adventures. A greedy and naughty space stowaway, Goober has the ability to change his colour and shape so is always jumping out and surprising Zip, Pella and Statz.

Zip's top tips

Zip and friends are here to help you talk in a fun new way - spell with your fingers and talk with your hands. Follow these top tips to get the most from their adventures:

- **Share the book together and enjoy the story**
- **Play with the signs**
- **Use Zip's alphabet to make your own words**
- **Visit Space School, enjoy the activities and have fun**
- **Watch out for Goober...**

SignSpell

Zip and the Big City Adventure

The spaceship has landed next to a very busy road.

The road has lots of lanes and there are lots of fast moving vehicles on it. "What are they?" asks Pella.

Statz looks at his Zablet. "When humans want to get places, they travel by car," he says. "Earth cars can only use a road. They don't hover like cruisers on planet Zee."

Road
Car
x2

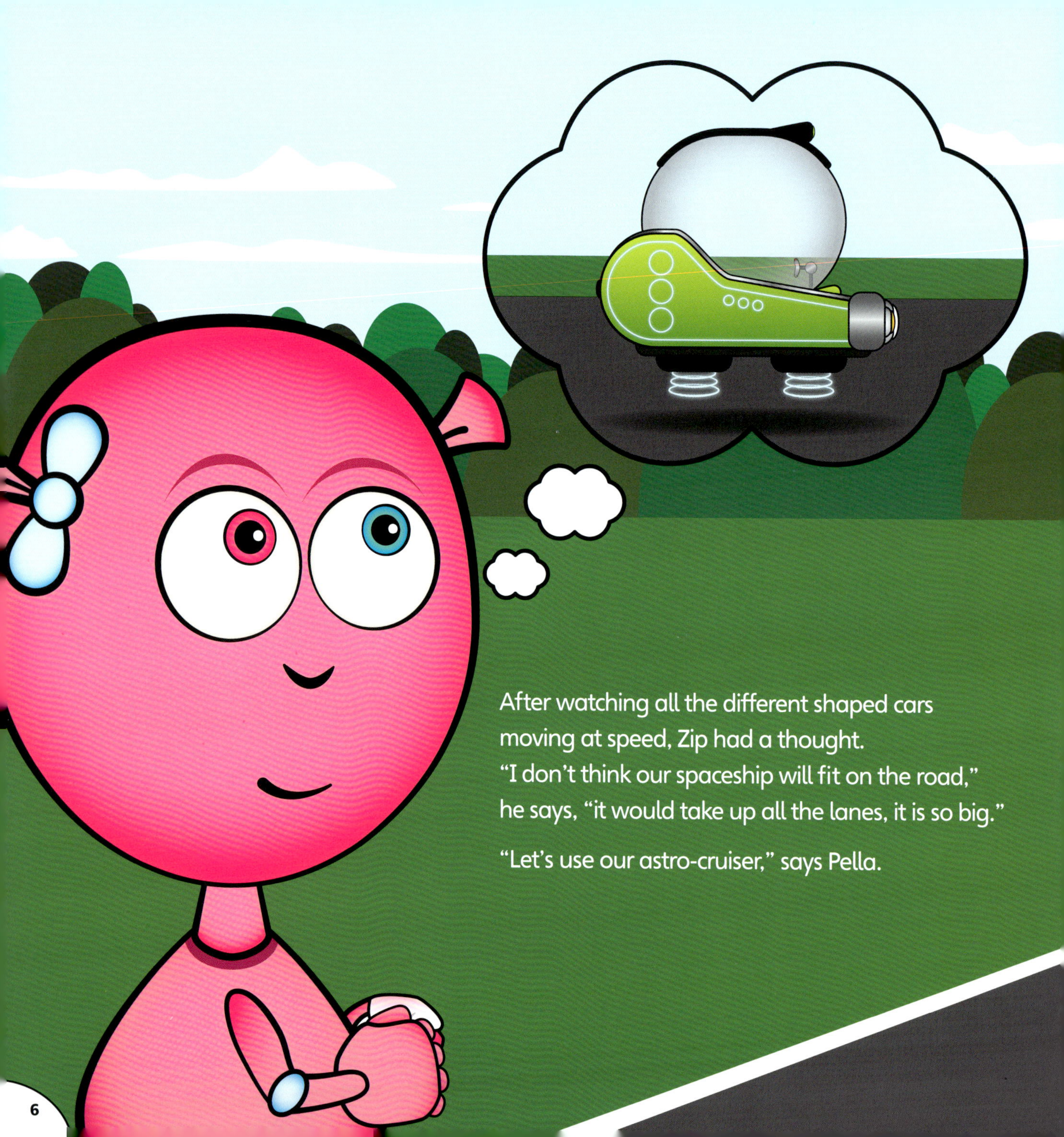

After watching all the different shaped cars moving at speed, Zip had a thought. "I don't think our spaceship will fit on the road," he says, "it would take up all the lanes, it is so big."

"Let's use our astro-cruiser," says Pella.

M1
Big City 32
Small Town 24
Tiny Village
A1609
½ m
03

"Where are the cars all going?" asks Pella.

"To the big city," says Statz. "Let's follow them and explore."

The friends unload their astro-cruiser from the spaceship. They get in and Pella steers them down the road towards the big city.

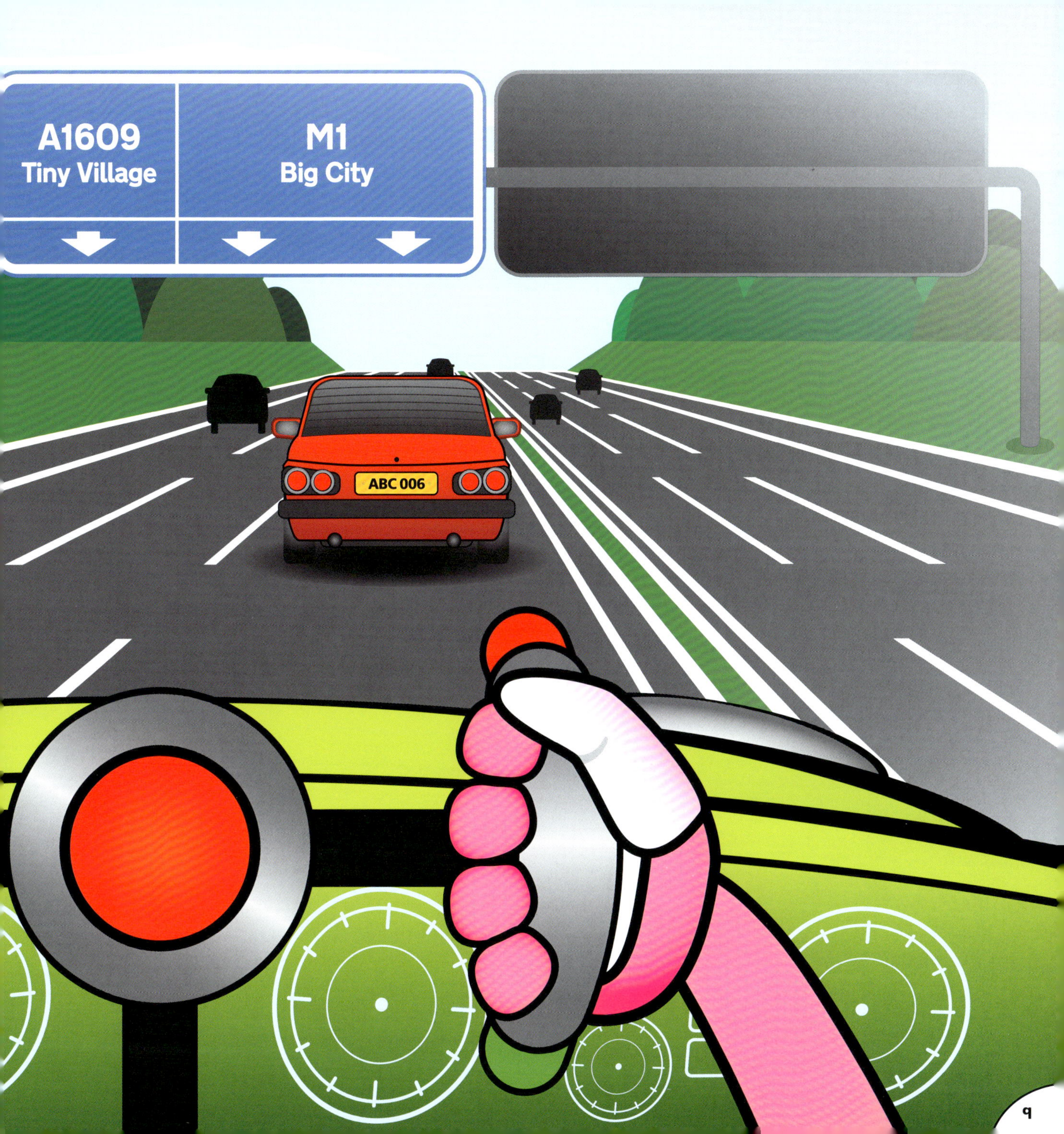
A1609
Tiny Village
M1
Big City
ABC 006

Zip sees the strangest car he has seen so far. “That car is flying,” says Zip, “I thought cars only drive on roads.”

“That is an aeroplane not a car. It flies to where it needs to go,” says Statz.

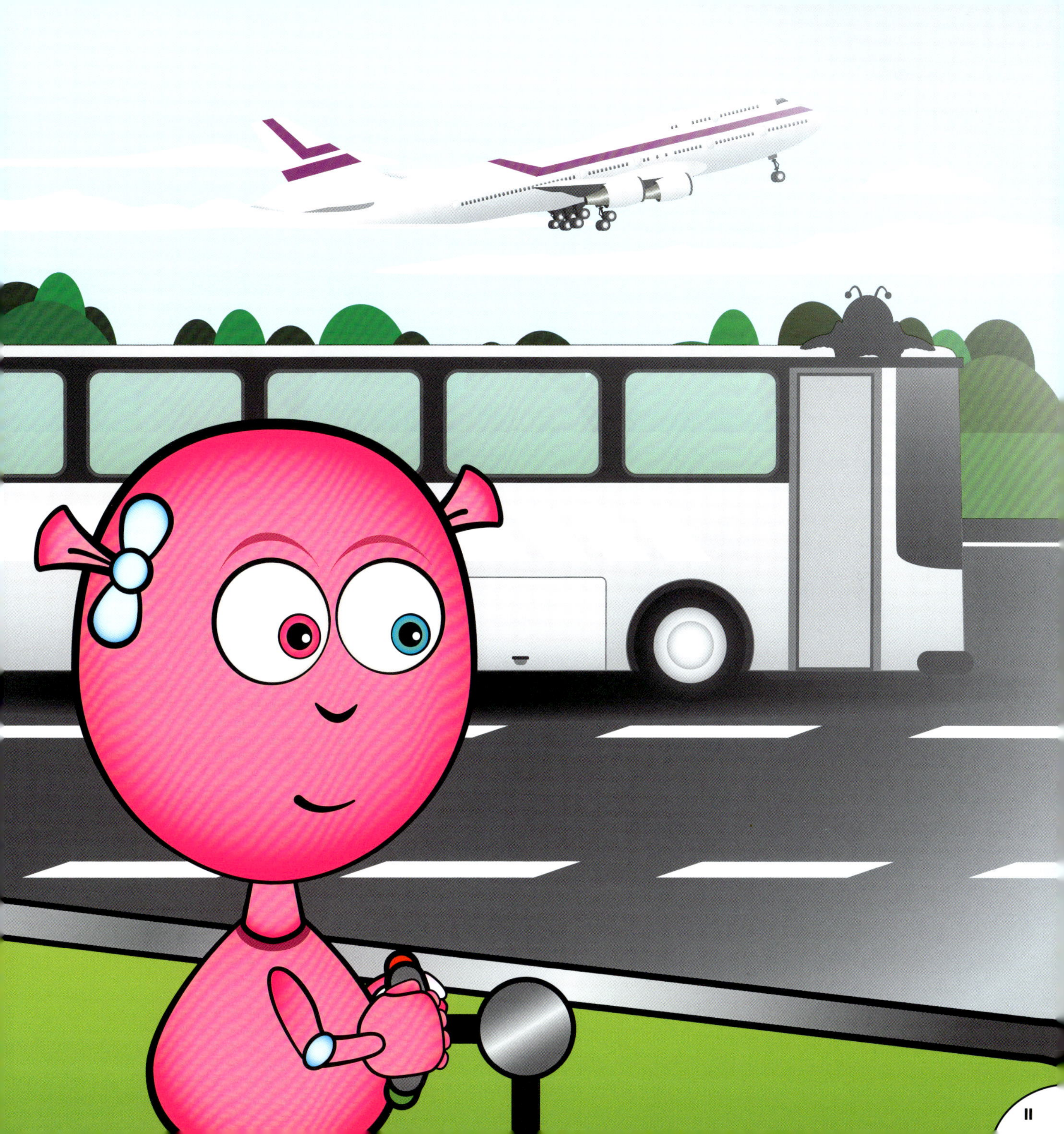

Zip, Pella and Statz soon slow down to a crawl. There is a queue of traffic waiting to get into the city.

"Look! There is a bus and it is travelling much faster than us," says Statz, "it has a lane of its own."

The friends decide that taking the bus would get them into the city quicker. They park the astro-cruiser and wait at the bus stop for their ride.

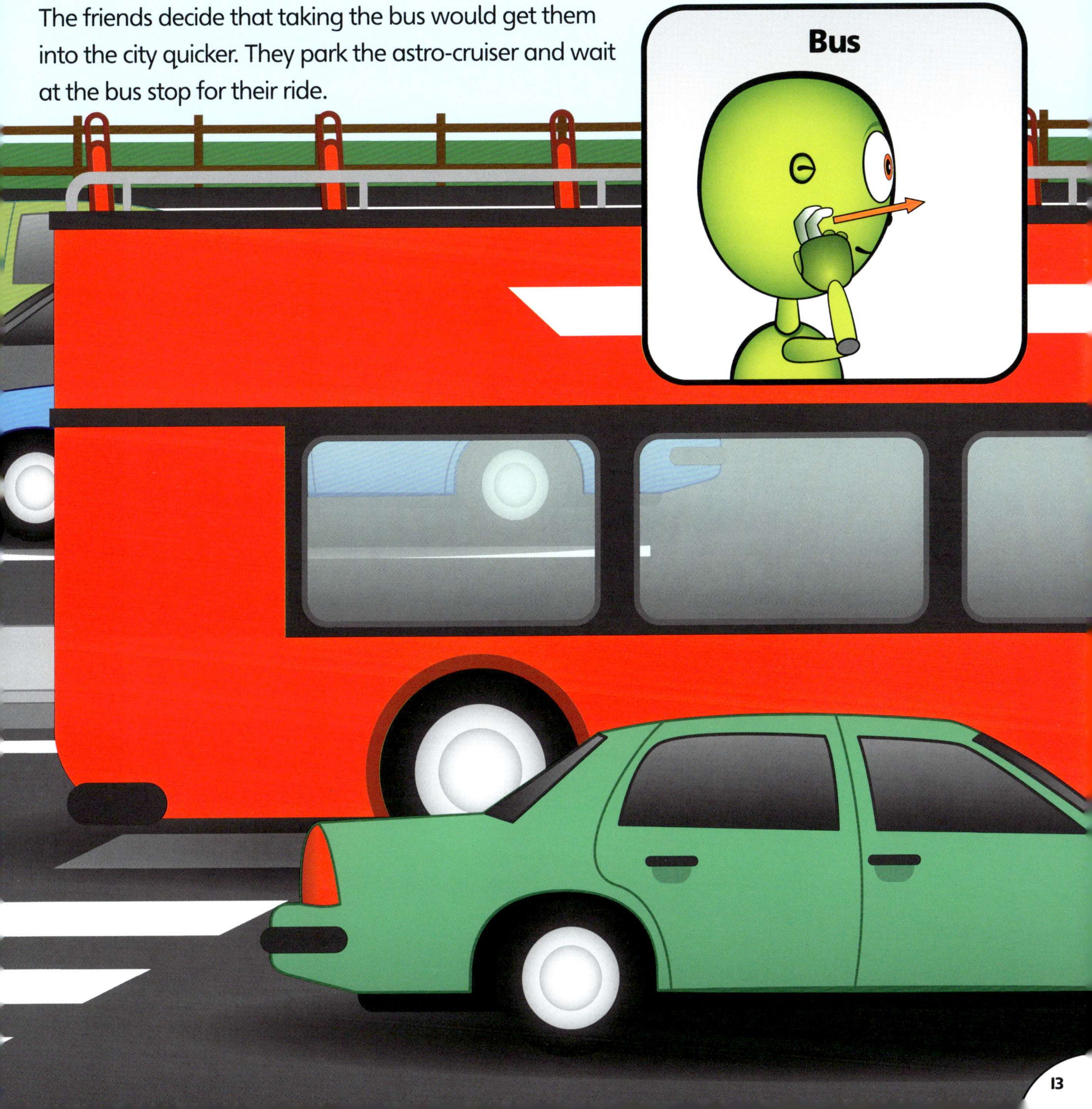

They buy their tickets from the bus driver and Zip races off up the stairs to the top deck.

Zip, Pella and Statz enjoy looking at the city sights from the bus.

"The bus is a great way to get around the city," says Statz. "We can see lots from here."

The friends see a giant wheel in the distance. "What does that do?" asks Pella.

"It lifts you up really high so you can see the whole city," says Statz.

The Big City Bus

Space School

Take a look at the pictures below.
See if you can spell each one using Zip's alphabet.

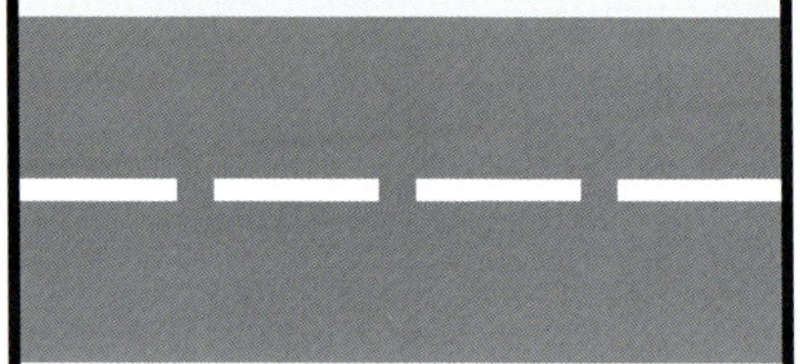

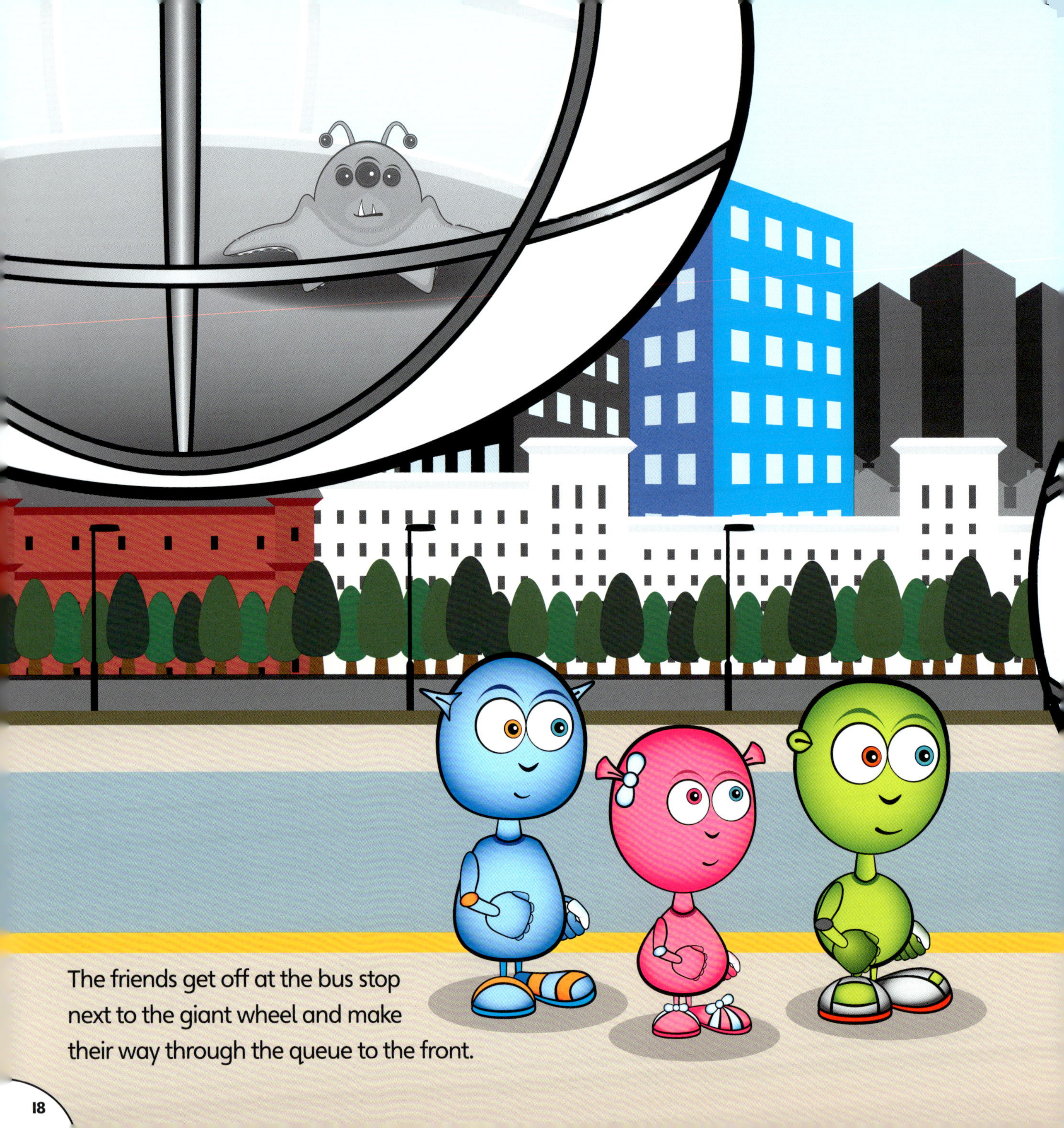

The friends get off at the bus stop
next to the giant wheel and make
their way through the queue to the front.

As the wheel turns, a pod door opens to let them in.
They pile inside and press their noses against the window.

The friends can see the whole city.

"From up here everything looks so small," says Zip.

Statz points to a boat on the river and Pella is amazed by a helicopter in the sky.

Once the wheel has turned all the way round, the friends get off.

"Wow, humans have lots of different ways to travel," says Zip.

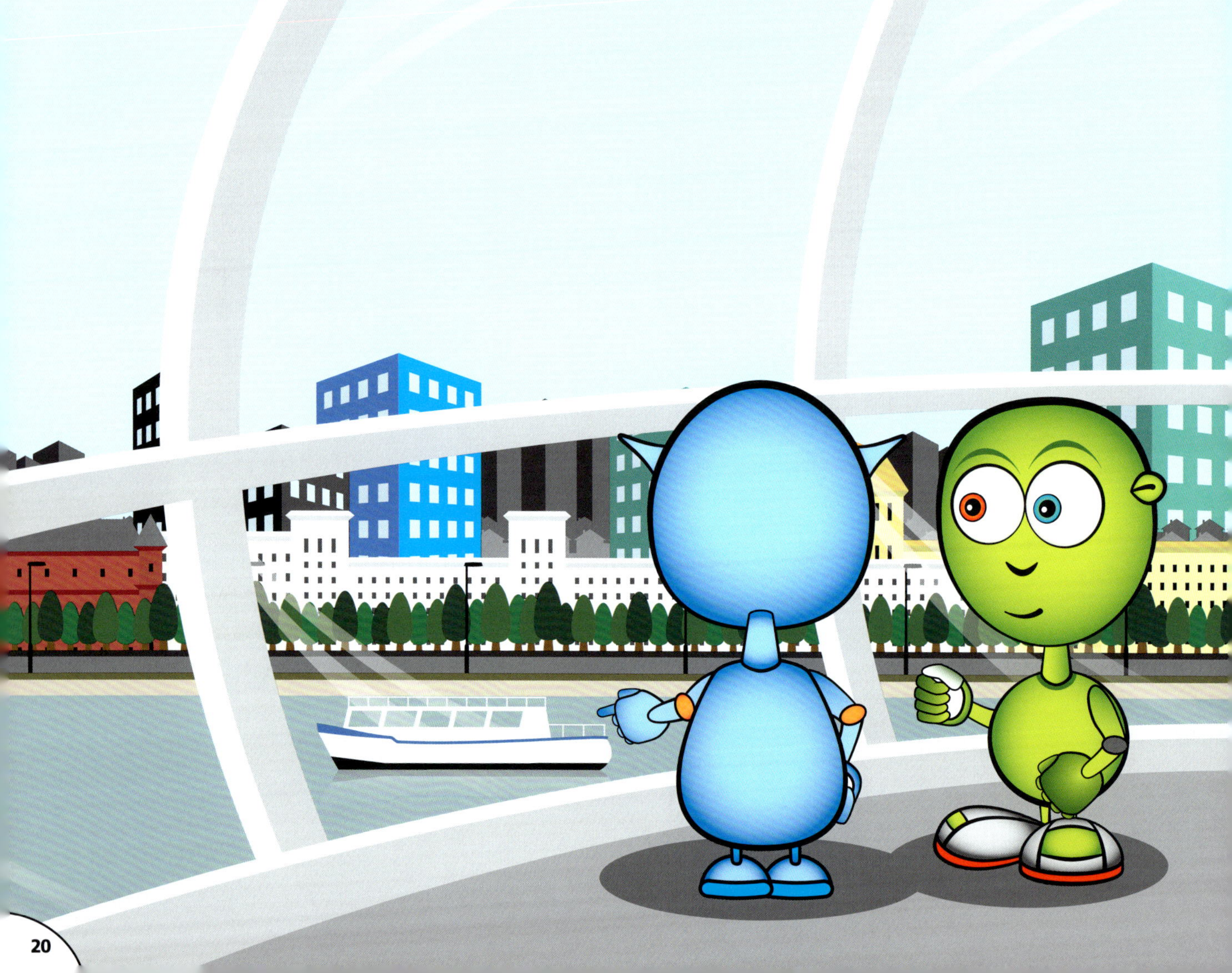

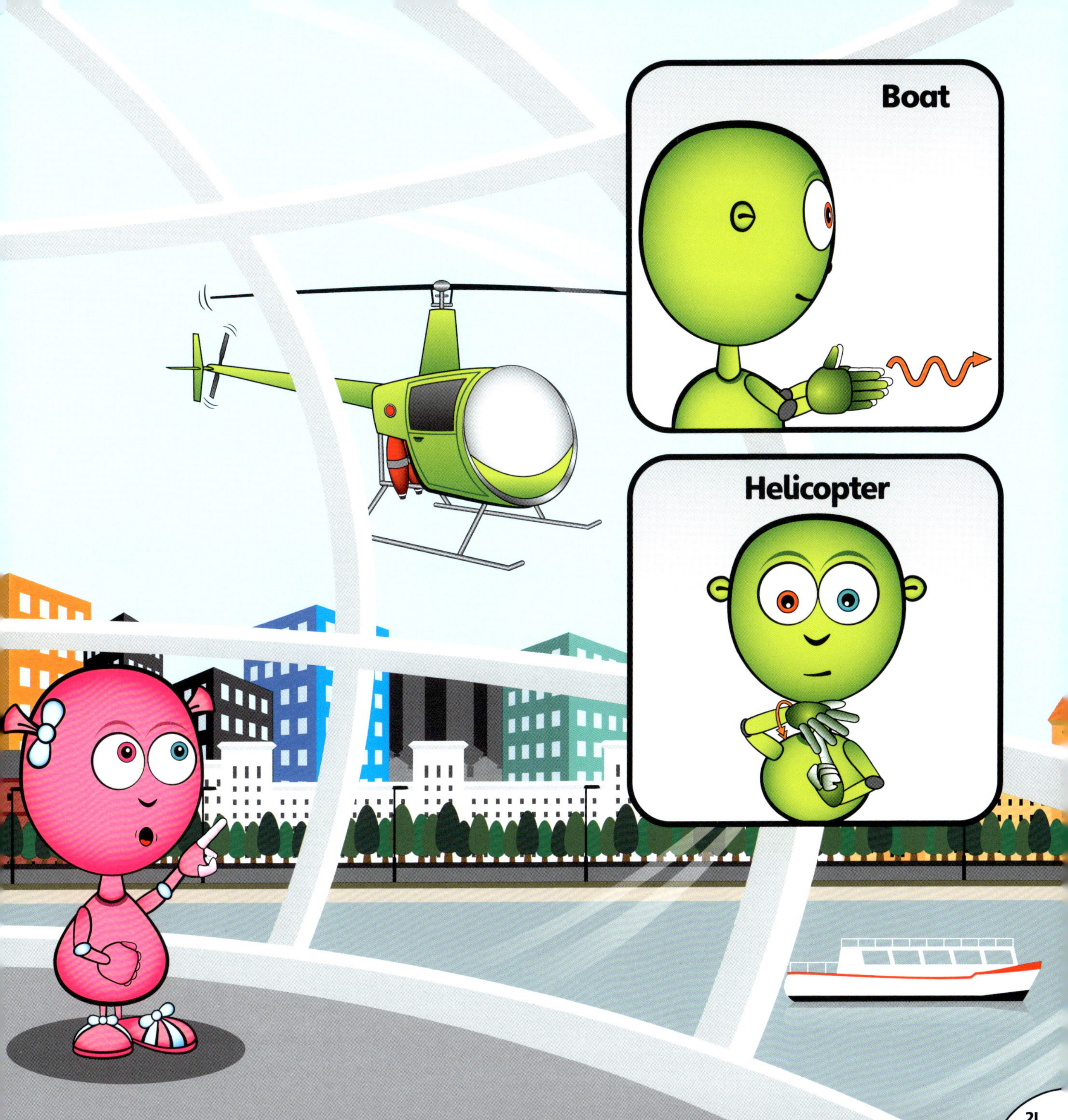
Boat
Helicopter

The friends are enjoying the sights and a nice walk across the big city.

Pella points to something on the other side of the road and a black car pulls up to where Pella's arm is held out. "Oops!" says Statz. "That is how you signal you would like a taxi."

Zip, Pella and Statz jump in the taxi and ask the driver to take them back to their astro-cruiser.

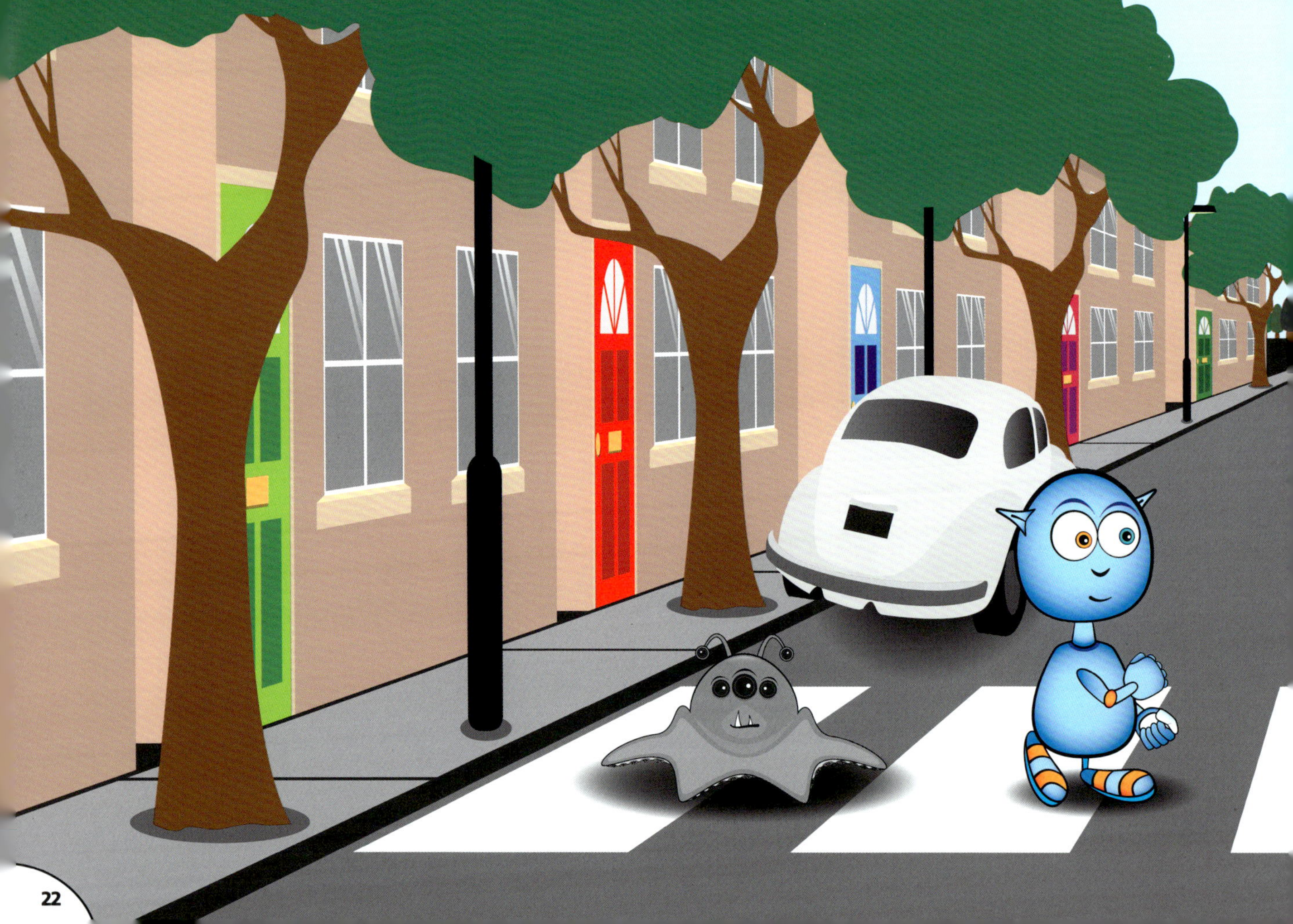

Walk
x2
Taxi
x2
TAXI
TAXI

The taxi weaves through the streets, turning left then right.

Then suddenly they stop. In front is a long queue of traffic.

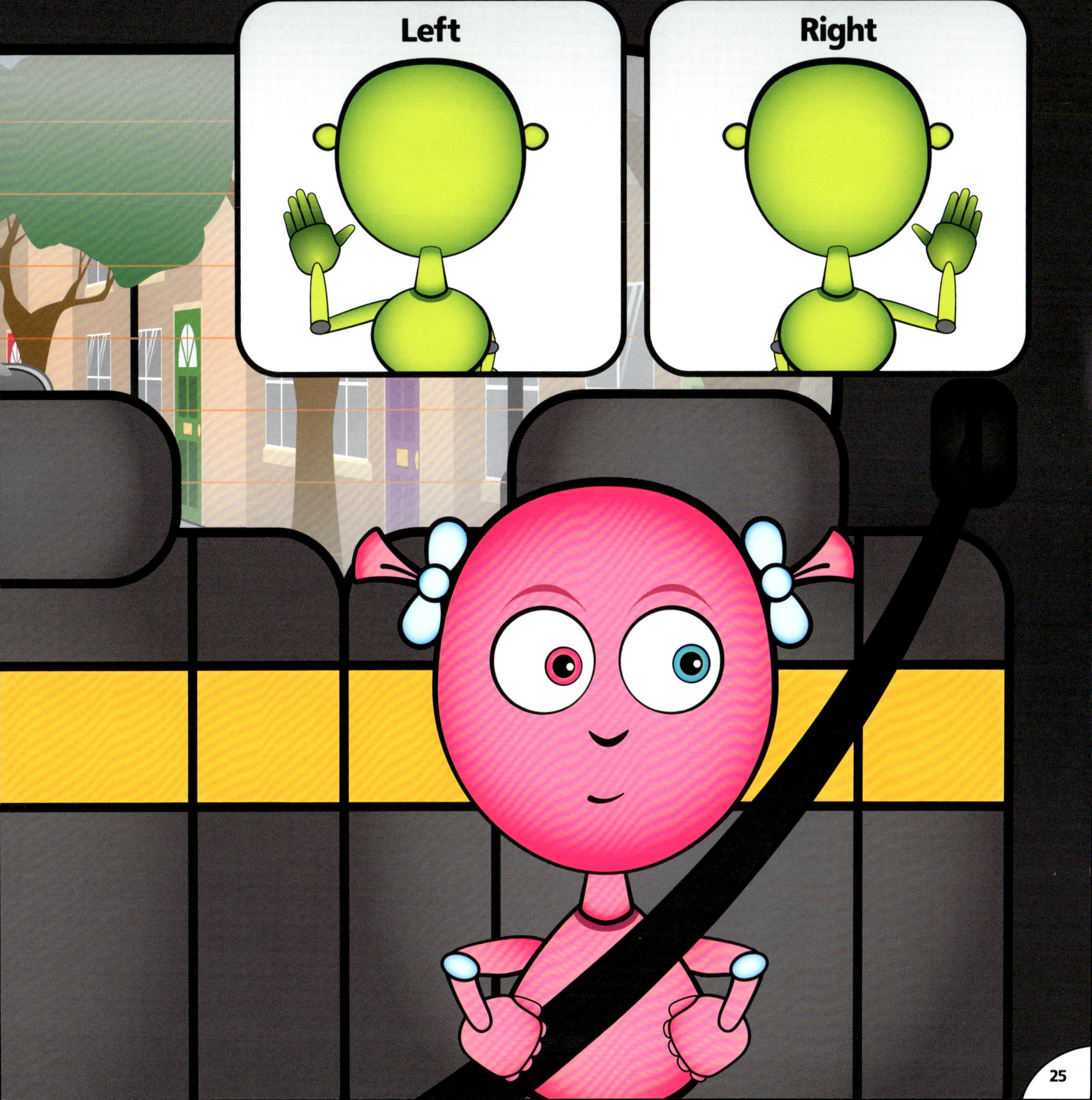
Left
Right

Space School

Zip has enjoyed the sights of the big city.
Can you remember how to sign the pictures below?

Boat

Helicopter

Taxi

Walking

Left

Right

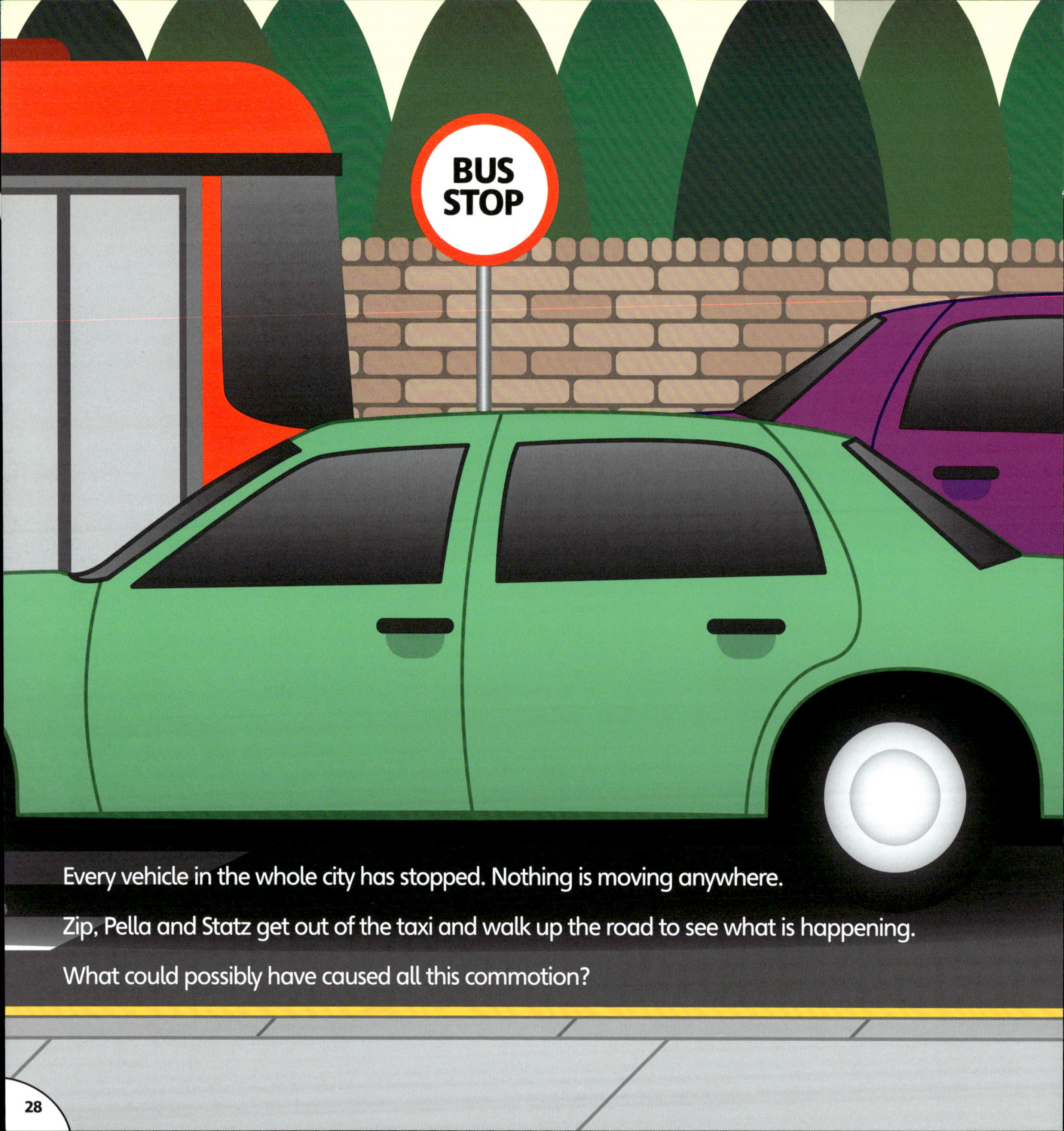

Every vehicle in the whole city has stopped. Nothing is moving anywhere.

Zip, Pella and Statz get out of the taxi and walk up the road to see what is happening.

What could possibly have caused all this commotion?

GOOBER!

Zip's Signs

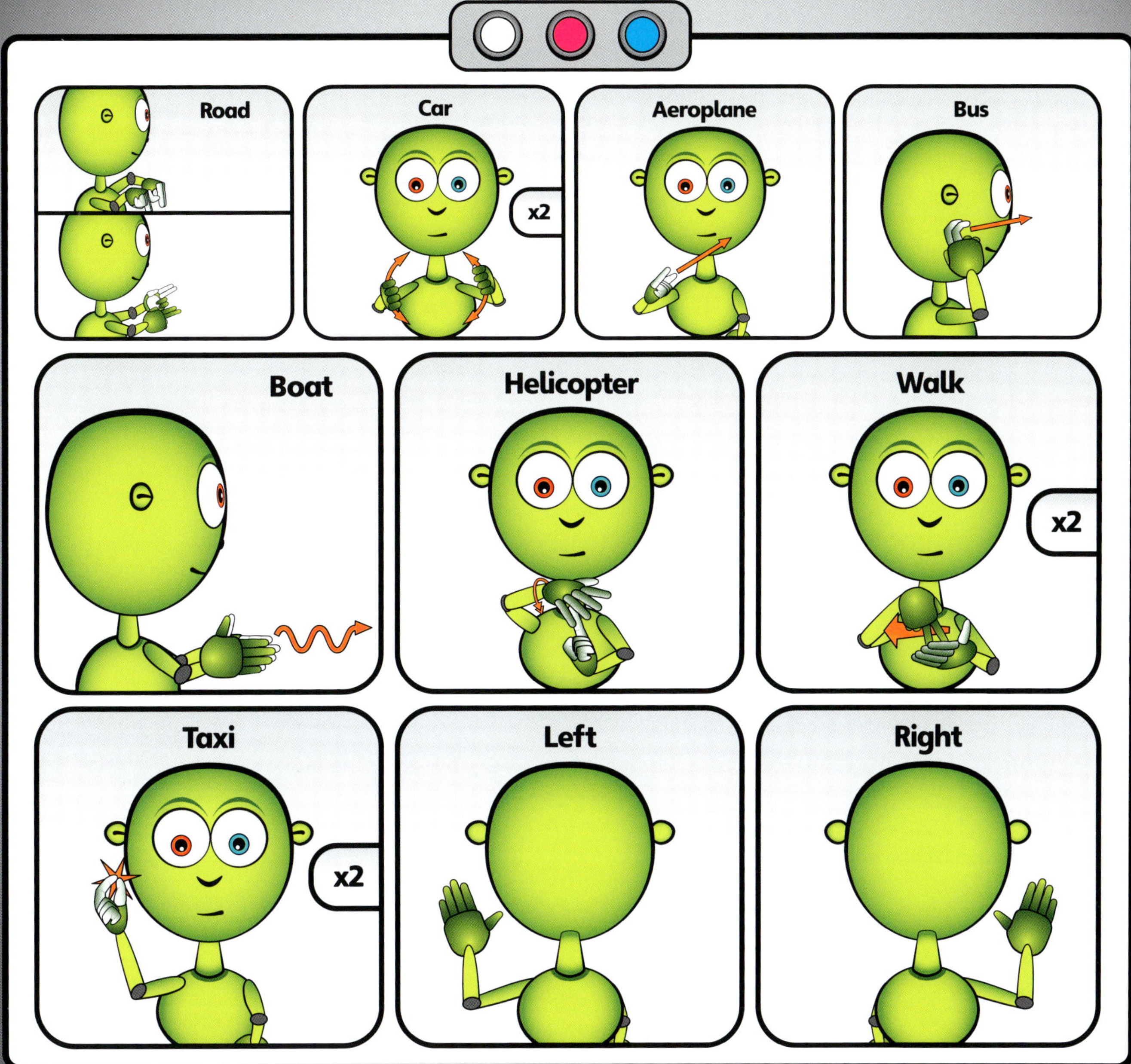

Road
Car
x2
Aeroplane
Bus
Boat
Helicopter
Walk
x2
Taxi
x2
Left
Right

Fun things to do

Now that you have read all about Zip and the Big City Adventure, here are some fun things for you to do...

- **Design your own astro-crusier - draw, describe or make**
- **How would you feel at the top of the giant wheel?**
- **Do you think travelling by car is a good idea?**
- **Which earth vehicle do you think Zip liked the most?**
- **What would you do if you were in a long queue of traffic?**
- **Teach a friend the sign for helicopter and how to spell it**

First published 2013 by Signature

SignSpell® stories created by Signature
Designed and illustrated by Igloo Imaging Ltd.